CW01512587

Original title:

Glassy Drifts Beyond the Mermaid Pulp

Copyright © 2025 Swan Charm

All rights reserved.

Author: Olivia Oja

ISBN HARDBACK: 978-1-80563-067-8

ISBN PAPERBACK: 978-1-80564-588-7

Liquid Tales from the Abyssal Plain

In shadows deep, where silence reigns,
Whispers of secrets, lost in chains.
Creatures dance in swirling gloom,
A world alive, yet steeped in doom.

Coral forests, ancient trees,
Swaying softly in murky breeze.
Echoes of laughter, muted calls,
Beneath the waves, a silence falls.

Softly glimmers, ghostly light,
Flickers dimly, a fleeting sight.
History clings to every scale,
In the depths, a forgotten tale.

Vast and endless, the ocean's hold,
Stories woven in colors bold.
From tempest storms to quiet nights,
Tales of the deep, of ancient sights.

Liquid tales, from ages past,
Memories anchored, forever cast.
In the abyss, where shadows play,
Life unfurls in a mysterious way.

Murmurs in the Nebula Sea

Stars dissolve in twilight's embrace,
Murmurs travel through time and space.
The echoes hum, a soothing tune,
Lost in the glow of a silver moon.

Nebula blooms in colors bright,
Whispers carried by cosmic light.
Galaxies shimmer, soft and grand,
Unraveling secrets, hand in hand.

Beneath the orbiting celestial dome,
Wanderers drift, far from home.
Each twinkling spark, a story told,
Of love and dreams, both brave and bold.

Ripples of thought by starlight stirred,
Carried on currents of light unheard.
Their secrets drift on a gentle breeze,
Murmurs linger in the stellar seas.

In this expanse, both wild and free,
Murmurs dance in the nebula sea.
A tapestry spun in endless night,
Where hope ignites in dazzling flight.

The Allure of the Shimmering Deep

Where sunlight kisses the ocean's crest,
Lies a world that calls, a hidden nest.
In hues of sapphire, visions bloom,
The shimmering deep, a siren's loom.

Bubbles rise like laughter's song,
Enticing hearts where dreams belong.
The embrace of water, cool and pure,
A secret place, both strange and sure.

Tides ebb and flow, in rhythmic dance,
Each wave a whisper, a fleeting chance.
Life pulses softly beneath the Blue,
Where every shimmer tells of the true.

From vibrant corals to shadows cast,
A tapestry woven, both present and past.
The allure of depths, so rich and vast,
Where time unravels, free from the fast.

The ocean breathes, a timeless plea,
In the heart of the deep, we long to be.
Embraced by wonders, lost in the sweep,
Of mysteries held in the shimmering deep.

Echoes of the Nautical Muse

On whispered winds, the sea's refrain,
Echoes drift across the main.
Tales of longing, lust, and lore,
Of sailors lost upon the shore.

With ink of waves, the pen does flow,
Capturing dreams from below.
Each stroke a journey, bold and free,
Guided by the nautical muse at sea.

Barnacles cling to weathered ships,
As moonlight bathes the ocean's lips.
Salt-kissed stories of bravery told,
In every voyage, the heart grows bold.

Beneath the surface, magic thrives,
In depths where the spirit of adventure dives.
Every echo whispers to the soul,
Calling forth the tides that make us whole.

The dance of waves, an ancient trance,
Inviting souls to take a chance.
In echoes soft, we heed the call,
The nautical muse, enchanting all.

Myths of the Abyss: Secrets Unfold

In shadows deep where silence dwells,
The whispers weave their aged spells.
Beneath the waves of endless night,
Ancient truths take wing in flight.

The sirens sing of dreams long lost,
Their haunting call, a treacherous cost.
With every note, the currents sway,
Dragging hearts to darkened gray.

In murky depths, where phantoms creep,
The secrets lie while watchers weep.
Glowing eyes in the dark recess,
Guard the tales that time must bless.

A shipwrecked soul, a fleeting spark,
Finds solace in the depths so stark.
From the abyss, a light shall rise,
To part the veil and claim the skies.

Awake the legends, let them soar,
Unlock the doors to ancient lore.
For in the sea, where dreams entwine,
The myths of the abyss forever shine.

The Siren's Heartbeat in the Mist

In twilight's grip, her song takes flight,
Soft whispers curling in the night.
A heart that calls from misty deep,
Where secrets slumber, lost in sleep.

The waves respond with soft caress,
A yearning pulse, the ocean's stress.
In every note, a tale unfolds,
Of love and loss, of dreams retold.

Her eyes, like stars, they shine so bright,
Guiding sailors through sheer fright.
Yet danger lurks in silken sound,
For those who linger, fate is found.

Beneath the foam, the shadows creep,
Where ancient spirits their vigil keep.
With every heartbeat, rhythms weave,
A siren's song, a web to deceive.

So heed the call of misty seas,
Let not your heart be swayed with ease.
For in the depths, enchantments lie,
A siren's love may be your tie.

Kaleidoscope of the Undersea Realm

Beneath the waves, a world anew,
Of colors bright and shadows blue.
Fish darting through a crystal maze,
In fleeting light, their beauty plays.

Coral castles rise with grace,
Guardians of this hidden place.
Tides weave stories in the sand,
A tapestry by nature's hand.

Seaweed sways like dancers fair,
In rhythms soft, through ocean air.
Each ripple tells of joy and strife,
A vibrant pulse of ocean life.

Echoes charm the depths so wide,
Whispers of the ocean's pride.
In swirling depths, a lively dream,
The sea's own heart, a glistening stream.

So dive into this realm so vast,
Where every moment holds its cast.
In kaleidoscopes of joy and fear,
The ocean breathes, forever near.

Memories from the Depths of Mermaids' Tears

In crystal pools where mermaids dwell,
Their laughter rings, a soothing bell.
Yet tears they shed for love forsaken,
In silent depths where dreams are shaken.

Each droplet holds a story's weight,
Of passions lost and destined fate.
In watery graves, they lay their dreams,
Where moonlight dances and starlight beams.

The currents pull at heartstrings tight,
A melody of wrong and right.
With every tear, a heart does break,
As shadows stir beneath the wake.

So listen close to ocean's sigh,
The echoes of a love gone by.
For in the depths, the mermaids' cries,
Are whispered secrets of the skies.

In twisted tales and hidden fears,
The ocean cradles mermaids' tears.
For love, once bright, can fade away,
Yet in their sorrows, hope will stay.

Fantasies Woven in Water's Embrace

In liquid dreams, the stories flow,
With every wave, new wonders grow.
A realm where myths and magic meld,
In water's arms, our dreams are held.

The silver fish, they dance and swirl,
As tides of fate begin to curl.
In every splash, a wish takes flight,
A glimpse of magic, pure delight.

Around the reefs, bright colors play,
In harmony, they weave the day.
Creatures twirl in joyful grace,
Fantasies born in water's embrace.

So close your eyes and drift away,
Let ocean's whispers guide your stay.
In every ripple, secrets hide,
Dreams and wishes, side by side.

For in this world of sea and light,
You'll find your heart takes joyous flight.
Within the depths, let magic stream,
Woven in every water's dream.

Secrets Lurking Near the Reefs

In shadows cast by coral bright,
Where colors dance in soft moonlight,
There lies a tale of old and new,
In depths unseen, the secret grew.

Fish weave stories through the tides,
While tangled weeds in silence bide,
A treasure lost, a whisper near,
The heart of ocean holds its dear.

Among the rocks, a siren's call,
Entices sailors with its thrall,
Enigmas hid in every swell,
Secrets that the waters tell.

Lurking shadows, mysteries deep,
A promise made, a promise to keep,
In every wave, in every breeze,
The ocean's voice brings minds to ease.

Awash in dreams, the tales unwind,
In whispered tales, the truth we find,
So dive beneath the ocean's hue,
And let the secrets speak to you.

A Canvas Painted by Ocean's Breath

Upon the shore, where waters kiss,
The azure waves in tranquil bliss,
A canvas bright, adorned with hue,
The ocean breathes, both bold and true.

With strokes of foam and whispers light,
It dances 'neath the stars at night,
Each wave a tale, each sigh a dream,
A masterpiece, a flowing stream.

Gentle tides, with rhythms rare,
Entwine the shores with tender care,
A palette vast, with hues profound,
In every ripple, magic's found.

The ocean sings, a siren's song,
As colors blend and drift along,
The sun dips low, the sky aglow,
In every brushstroke, wonders flow.

With every surge, a story spun,
Of storms endured and battles won,
A living art, forever stretched,
By ocean's breath, our hearts are etched.

Enigmas of the Shimmering Depths

Where sunlight fades and shadows play,
The depths conceal what words can't say,
An enigma wrapped in swirling blue,
The ocean's heart beats bold and true.

Creatures glide in silken grace,
In silent halls, they find their place,
A world beneath, where few have seen,
In every wave, a hidden dream.

Ancient ships in slumber rest,
Guarding treasures, lost and blessed,
Their stories echo through the gloom,
In watery halls, their tales resume.

The shimmering depths, a secret domain,
Where laughter dances and ghosts remain,
Seekers roam with hearts aflame,
In pursuit of fortune, love, and fame.

Yet quiet whispers, soft and low,
Urge caution here, the depths bestow,
An enigma framed in liquid light,
In ocean's hold, both day and night.

Whispers through the Surf of Time

In every crash, a tale anew,
The whispers weave like morning dew,
Through surf that kisses golden sand,
Time flows gently, hand in hand.

The ocean breathes a timeless rhyme,
Each wave a moment, each grain of time,
Echoes of laughter and forlorn sighs,
As memories dance beneath the skies.

The secrets carved by wind and tide,
In hues of blue where dreams abide,
A symphony of ebb and flow,
A cosmic clock in rhythmic show.

With every roll, the stories swell,
Of lovers lost and wishes fell,
Through fog and light, we drift and roam,
The sea, a whisper, calls us home.

So listen close, for time will share,
The wisdom wrapped in salty air,
For in the surf, a truth takes flight,
Through whispers soft, we find our light.

Serenade of the Luminous Ocean's Edge

Beneath the waves where secrets hide,
The moonlight dances, a guide to the tide.
Whispers of waves call out to the shore,
While starfish twinkle, forevermore.

Salted winds carry tales of old,
Of mariners brave and treasures untold.
The ocean breathes in rhythms sweet,
A serenade where hearts can meet.

Shells adorned with glittering hues,
Embrace the night with shimmering views.
With every crest and gentle lull,
The deep unfolds its magic, a pull.

Secrets swirl in the sapphire deep,
Where time stands still and dreams can seep.
The luminous waves sing soft refrains,
A melody echoing through the plains.

In the embrace of the ocean's call,
We know the tide will catch us all.
A serenade beneath the skies,
Where love and wonder never dies.

Dreamscapes within Aquatic Dreams

In realms where the water and visions blend,
The fish weave tales that never end.
Coral castles rise and fall,
In a starlit dream where echoes call.

Bubbles dance, like laughter in light,
Crafting illusions that sparkle bright.
Mermaids weave spells, both tender and bold,
In aquatic dreams, more precious than gold.

Each droplet holds a story long,
Of ancient kingdoms and forgotten song.
Swirls of color, vibrant and free,
Unlocking realms for the heart to see.

Waves carry whispers from long ago,
The turbulent depths where hopes will flow.
In shadowy depths, the secrets reside,
In aquatic dreams, we find our guide.

So dive deep into the azure sea,
Where dreams awaken and spirits flee.
A beckoning call, a soft embrace,
In the dance of water, we find our place.

Chanterelle of the Enchanted Abyss

In the shadows where silence looms,
The chanterelle blooms in watery tombs.
A symphony hidden beneath the wave,
Echoing secrets of the briny grave.

Gold and silver glint in the dark,
As sea creatures gather, a shimmering spark.
The abyss sings with a haunting tune,
Beneath the glow of a ghostly moon.

Each note a tale of wonders spun,
Of merfolk dancing, of battles won.
The depths pulse with the magic's flow,
A chant that the bravest dare to know.

In the coral gardens, wisdom waits,
A treasure chest filled with fates.
Chanterelles whisper, a soft refrain,
In the enchanted depths, love does remain.

So seek the shadows where dreams reside,
With the ebbing tide as your guide.
In the heart of the abyss, find the light,
Where the chanterelle beckons with delight.

Refractions of the Enigmatic Waters

In the glassy surface, mysteries swirl,
Reflections dancing in a watery whirl.
The depths conceal what the eye can't see,
An enigmatic world, wild and free.

Ripples shimmer with secrets profound,
As echoes of laughter pulse all around.
Each wave a story, each ripple a sigh,
Beneath the blue, where dreams can fly.

Azure wilds hold the wise and daft,
Their voices guided by the ocean's draft.
As sunlight fractures in radiant hues,
The waters reveal what the heart imbues.

Fathoms deep, where shadows do play,
Magic and mystery dance all day.
In swirling eddies, life's currents enfold,
Enigmatic waters, a sight to behold.

So gaze upon the sea's embrace,
Let the tides take you to a lingering place.
For in the refractions, treasures await,
In the waters' own dance, we create our fate.

Enigma of the Aquatic Veil

In the depths where shadows dwell,
A jade enchantress casts her spell.
With whispers soft, the secrets rise,
A dance beneath the watery skies.

Veils of mist weave tales of old,
Of treasures lost and dreams untold.
The currents swirl, a gentle sigh,
Embracing all who dare to dive.

Bubbles break like fleeting thoughts,
In the silent depths, time forgot.
Each flicker of light a distant star,
Guiding lost souls, near and far.

Glimmers of hope in a vast expanse,
Where vibrant life joins in the dance.
An ancient lore that ebbs and flows,
Unlocking paths where magic grows.

What riddles lie in realms unseen?
Each turn a promise, bright and keen.
The aquatic veil, a world so grand,
Awaits the brave, the bold, the hand.

Celestial Currents and Ocean's Breath

Beneath a sky of azure hue,
The ocean breathes with secrets new.
Celestial currents twist and turn,
In every wave, a flame does burn.

The tides, they whisper ancient lore,
Of shipwrecks lost on sandy shore.
In moonlit glow, the waters gleam,
Carrying hopes on a silver stream.

A symphony of salt and spray,
Each crash of wave a soft ballet.
Stars reflect on liquid glass,
Holding the night as moments pass.

From depths below to skies above,
The ocean sings of life and love.
In every ripple, a tale unfolds,
Of treasures found and dreams retold.

With every breath, the sea inspires,
A spark of magic that never tires.
In the dance of currents, we must trust,
For in the ocean's heart, we are dust.

Serenade of the Coral Garden

In the garden where corals bloom,
Life bursts forth, dispelling gloom.
Colors dance in vibrant hues,
A palette rich with nature's muse.

Gentle waves caress each flower,
Life thrives in this hidden bower.
Fish dart like thoughts in joyful streams,
Amongst the reefs, they weave their dreams.

The serenade of ocean's song,
Plays softly where the heart belongs.
With every note, a spark ignites,
Bringing forth days and starry nights.

Beneath the sun's warm golden gaze,
Each creature sways in watery maze.
A sanctuary, wild and free,
The coral garden, eternity.

Whispers echo in hushed tones,
Within this realm, no one is alone.
As life unfolds beneath the tide,
In coral's arms, we too will hide.

Whispers from the Deep Blue

From the deep where shadows creep,
Comes a voice from waters deep.
In hushed tones, the secrets flow,
Of ancient ones, and tales we know.

The ocean's heart, a thrum of dreams,
In every wave, the starlight beams.
A lingered touch, a fleeting sigh,
In every crest and every sigh.

Beneath the veil of moonlit grace,
Life dances in a tender space.
From trembling kelp to dancing ray,
They share the language of the spray.

These whispers beckon, calling near,
To brave the depths, to face the fear.
For in each current lies the truth,
A promise kept since distant youth.

So listen close, embrace the night,
For every shadow gives off light.
In the deep blue's tender embrace,
We find our home, our sacred place.

Twilight Musings on Submerged Shores

In twilight's glow, the shadows dance,
Whispers carry on the sea's expanse.
The tides sing secrets from ages past,
Where dreams of sailors in silence last.

Beneath the waves, the treasures lie,
Cradled softly, where memories sigh.
Shells of wisdom, pearls of grace,
Reveal the stories time can't erase.

A lighthouse stands, its beacon bright,
Guiding lost souls through the night.
Stars above flicker with glee,
As they watch over the tranquil sea.

And as the sun dips low and rare,
The ocean's heart lays itself bare.
With every crest, each gentle swell,
Lies a tale that the waters tell.

So linger here, on this shore divine,
Where sun and moon in rhythm align.
In twilight's arms, let thoughts take flight,
As dreams of submerged shores ignite the night.

Echoes of the Drowned Paradise

Listen close to the ocean's breath,
It carries tales of love and death.
Where once we danced on golden sand,
Now echoes linger, hand in hand.

Ruins rise in the depths so blue,
Whispers of a world we once knew.
Fragments of laughter, echoes of song,
In the stillness, they linger long.

Ghostly ships on the horizon fade,
Bearing the dreams that never strayed.
Fathoms deep in the silent air,
Haunted souls find solace there.

With every wave, the memories surge,
Of vibrant life and love's sweet urge.
A paradise lost, yet never gone,
In the heart of the sea, it lingers on.

So listen well, let the waters speak,
Of bright tomorrows and futures bleak.
In the depths, a promise waits,
Echoes of paradise, the ocean's gates.

Soliloquies in the Coral Abyss

In the coral gardens, silence reigns,
Where vibrant life its beauty gains.
Whispers of nature, soft and low,
Sing of wonders that ebb and flow.

Colors entwine in a dance of grace,
Each fish a brushstroke in this space.
Anemones sway to the ocean's song,
In the abyss where all belongs.

Listen to the heartbeat of the sea,
Each pulse a reminder of what can be.
Mysteries lurk in the shadows cast,
Voices of ancients, futures amassed.

Dancing light through the depths does peek,
Illuminating secrets that softly speak.
In the sacred stillness, thoughts do drift,
As the ocean cradles each precious gift.

So wander deeply, lose yourself there,
In the coral abyss, without a care.
Let the silence wrap you in embrace,
And find the beauty in time and space.

Enigmas of the Undulating Sea

The sea undulates with secrets old,
A tapestry of tales untold.
With every wave, a riddle spins,
Whispers of journeys where time begins.

Mariners lost in the misty blue,
Chasing the shadows of dreams that flew.
A compass turns, yet still they roam,
In the embrace of an oceanic home.

What lies beneath the rolling crest?
Visions of wonders, a sailor's quest.
Echoes of laughter, ghosts in the spray,
The ocean hums where spirits play.

A star-lit sky reflects on the tide,
An enigmatic dance, a celestial guide.
Dive into depths where mysteries wade,
And find the magic in the glades.

So float on waves of a cerulean hue,
Let the sea's whispers awaken you.
With open hearts and minds set free,
We'll unravel the enigmas of the sea.

Whispers of the Ocean's Soul

In twilight's embrace, the sea whispers near,
With secrets of ages, both distant and clear.
Waves dance on the shore, a rhythmic ballet,
Where wishes are born, then drift far away.

Stars twinkle softly, like dreams in the night,
Painting the water with silver and light.
Each ripple a story, each bubble a sigh,
As the tide carries echoes, of days gone by.

The breeze carries laughter, the salt in the air,
An orchestra playing, a song to declare.
With shells as the chorus, and gulls in the choir,
The ocean breathes life, igniting desire.

Adventures lie waiting in depths unexplored,
Where shadows and wonders are lovingly stored.
From coral gardens to vast sapphire halls,
The ocean, it beckons, to answer its calls.

So listen for whispers when twilight is nigh,
For tales of the deep, as the world says goodbye.
Embrace the enchantment, the magic it sows,
In whispers of the ocean, the heart ever knows.

The Submerged Ballet of Light

In ocean's embrace, the dancers take flight,
With glimmers of silver and strokes of soft white.
Beneath the blue veil, where shadows do play,
The ballet of light weaves dreams into day.

They twirl with the currents, a shimmering grace,
As sunlight cascades and kisses each face.
An intricate waltz with the tides as their guide,
In this underwater realm, where wonders reside.

The flicker of fin, the whisper of glee,
A harmony woven in depths of the sea.
With seagrass as partners, they swirl and they sway,
In a mesmerizing dance, where time fades away.

Each ripple a note in this symphonic sea,
The ocean's own heartbeat, a pure melody.
A concert of colors, of life intertwined,
Where magic and mystery await to be mined.

So join in the waltz, let your spirit take flight,
With the submerged ballet, in the stillness of night.
For in every dark corner, a glimmer will shine,
Where dreams meet the depths, and the heart feels divine.

Dreams Cradled in the Waves

Upon the soft shore, where the ocean doth sigh,
Dreams float on the surface, like clouds in the sky.
Each wave a soft cradle, each swell a warm kiss,
A lullaby whispered, of sweet, fleeting bliss.

The tides hold the secrets of oceans unknown,
With treasures that sparkle, like stars overgrown.
In shells held like wishes, the echoes remain,
Of time spent in reverie, free from all pain.

The sun dips to slumber, painting skies red,
While night casts its blanket, of dreams softly spread.
With every breath taken, the waves start to spin,
A dance of remembrance, where joy waits within.

Beneath the calm surface, where shadows reside,
The heartbeats of stories and sorrows confide.
For dreams cradle gently in waters so deep,
Where mermen sing softly, and mermaids dare leap.

So let the waves carry your hopes on their wings,
As the ocean embraces, the magic it brings.
In dreams cradled softly, beneath moonlit skies,
The tides weave enchantment, where fantasy lies.

Sonnet of the Luminous Depths

In depths of the ocean, where dreams intertwine,
A sonnet of light through the shadows doth shine.
With flickers of magic igniting the dark,
The chorus of colors ignites a bright spark.

From corals that blush, to the fish that do dart,
Each heartbeat a rhythm, a dance of the heart.
The depths hold the whispers of stories untold,
Where wonders, like tapestry, slowly unfold.

The moon's silver gaze on the waters does play,
As the ocean hums softly, a lullaby's sway.
Each wave sings of secrets, both tender and bold,
A sonnet of life in the deep that we hold.

Through currents and eddies, the spirit must roam,
In luminous depths, the sea calls us home.
With echoes of laughter, with love and with strife,
The ocean composes the symphony of life.

So dive in the depths, where the heart knows to flow,
For the sonnet of light shines the way we must go.
In every soft ripple, in every deep sigh,
The ocean's sweet song is a promise to lie.

Veils of Aqua Dreams

In the hush of twilight's grace,
Whispers drift through the space.
Like ribbons spun from moonlit lace,
Shadows dance in a gentle embrace.

Bubbles rise from depths below,
Tales of tides begin to flow.
With every shimmer, secrets grow,
In this realm where dreamers go.

Coral crowns and pebbled stones,
Cradled soft in ocean's tones.
Mysteries wrapped in soft moans,
Guarded by the sea's old drones.

Fields of kelp sway with delight,
As starlit fish take to flight.
In tranquility, all feels right,
Underneath the silver light.

So let the waves their stories weave,
In aqua dreams one can believe.
For in the depths, hearts will cleave,
To the wonders oceans conceive.

The Cascading Secrets of the Deep

Torn from the seams of gentle waves,
Lie the secrets that the sea saves.
In whispers soft, through water caves,
Time spins stories that time braves.

Currents twist and twirl with grace,
Carving paths, a liquid trace.
In the depths, a wild chase,
For the spirits that embrace.

Echoes call from shadows near,
What lies beneath, we hold dear.
In the dark, there's naught to fear,
For the whispers hearts will hear.

Bright horizons blend with the gloom,
Where vibrant blooms in silence bloom.
The ocean guards its secret room,
With each tide's rise, we are entombed.

So take heed of each soft sigh,
As waves hold truths we can't deny.
For in the deep, the old gods lie,
In the secrets they devise.

Reflection in the Mermaid's Pool

Stillness holds the evening's breath,
Where water reflects like enchanted death.
Soft ripples play like thoughts bereft,
In the pool, where dreams are deft.

Mermaids sing with haunting grace,
Each note a spark in this quiet space.
They beckon souls to join their chase,
In the depths their secrets trace.

Silver scales beneath the moon,
Glistening bright, a calling tune.
Dancing shadows break the gloom,
In this pool, strange futures loom.

Fingers skim through liquid glass,
In reflections of ages past.
With every splash, a spell is cast,
In the dreams that linger, vast.

So lean close to the pool's embrace,
And find the beauty time can't erase.
For in its depths, we find our place,
In the whispers, and the grace.

The Elegy of the Forgotten Sea

Once a cradle of nature's song,
Now a whisper, fading, strong.
Where tides once swayed, now they're wrong,
In memories, the sea belongs.

Ghostly ships on horizons weep,
Echoes of promises we keep.
As time slips by, shadows creep,
Through the depths where secrets sleep.

Sands of gold now turned to grey,
Ripples of laughter drift away.
In the elegance of decay,
We mourn the beauty that won't stay.

Lost in the thrum of silent night,
Where sailors' souls take tender flight.
The elegy floats, a bittersweet rite,
For the treasures hidden from our sight.

So heed the tales of water's sigh,
For beneath the stars, secrets lie.
In the heart of the sea, we cry,
An elegy to the truth we deny.

In the Embrace of the Celestial Sea

Beneath the stars, the waves do sing,
Whispers of dreams, to the night they cling.
A gentle tide, a lullaby's grace,
Stars woven tight in the ocean's embrace.

Moonlight dances on the water's face,
An endless expanse, a timeless space.
Each crest and trough, a tale untold,
In the depths of blue, the magic unfolds.

Secrets unfurl like petals in bloom,
Guided by starlight, dispelling the gloom.
On this celestial path, we find our way,
In the embrace of the night, we'll forever stay.

Secrets of the Liquid Abyss

Down in the depths, where shadows creep,
Lies a world of wonders, in silence, they sleep.
Mysteries dwell in the cold, dark void,
Treasures untold, waiting to be enjoyed.

Whispers of secrets in bubbles rise,
Echoes of creatures in the ocean's guise.
From corals that glow to the grandest of whales,
Each heartbeat pulses with ancient tales.

Journey below where the sky's lost sight,
In a kingdom of shades, where day meets night.
The liquid abyss holds stories profound,
In its haunting embrace, enchantments abound.

The Unseen Journey of the Ocean's Heart

Hidden below in a world so deep,
Lies the ocean's heart, a secret to keep.
Currents that pull, like a lover's embrace,
Nativity of wonders, in a watery space.

Drifting along, the tides weave their tale,
Carried by whispers that never grow stale.
The dance of the waves, a rhythmic delight,
Guiding the lost through the shroud of night.

In the swell of the sea, life starts anew,
A symphony played as the waters construe.
The unseen journey, profound and vast,
Flowing through time, connecting all past.

Voices Carried by Salty Breezes

Across the shores, where dreams collide,
Salty breezes carry tales of the tide.
Songs of the seabirds, a joyful refrain,
In the windswept whispers, love shall remain.

The sun dips low, painting skies afire,
Promises of tomorrow, wrapped in desire.
Each gust a memory, fleeting and sweet,
Echoing laughter where land and sea meet.

In every breath, the ocean's breath sings,
Casting a spell on the soul it clings.
Voices of the deep, with secrets they weave,
In salty breezes, our hearts will believe.

Notes from the Ocean's Heartstrings

Beneath the waves, where secrets dwell,
Coral castles cast their spell.
Whispers drift through salty air,
Siren songs of love and care.

Hushed melodies of bright fish glide,
In this realm, their dreams abide.
The moon weaves silver in the tide,
As night's embrace becomes a guide.

Wanderers of the deep take flight,
With lanterns bright, they chase the light.
In the pulse of the sea so grand,
Lives the magic of this land.

Echoes of laughter, soft and sweet,
Lost treasures in the sand we greet.
With each wave, the heart expands,
A symphony at nature's hands.

The Dance of Shadows beneath the Tides

In twilight's hush, shadows play,
Beneath the surf, they swirl and sway.
Dancing light on a phantom stage,
Ocean's dreams, a timeless page.

Crabs scuttle on their nightly quest,
While gentle waves find their rest.
The stars glance down with knowing eyes,
As whispered moonbeams kiss the skies.

In underwater balls, they twine,
Fluid forms in a ballet divine.
Each ripple tells a tale untold,
Of shipwrecked hopes and treasures bold.

Through kelp forests, shadows glide,
In this realm, they fate collide.
The dance continues, ebb and flow,
A secret world where few can go.

Atlantis' Whisper in the Flow

Ancient echoes, tales divine,
From sunken lands where dreams entwine.
Atlantis calls with a voice so clear,
In the currents, we feel it near.

Beneath the waves, history veils,
With shimmering shells and ghostly trails.
Soft caresses of the sea's embrace,
Awaken the past in this forgotten place.

Through coral halls, lost voices sing,
Lulling the heart with eternal spring.
A treasure bright in every tear,
Of love, of loss, they persevere.

Glimmers of gold in the deep reside,
Where fate and fortune gently collide.
Each ripple holds an ancient tale,
In the whispers of winds that sail.

Rhythms of the Enchanted Ocean

In the heart of the sea, rhythms beat,
With tides that dance, they move with heat.
An ocean's pulse sings soft and low,
Where secrets long to ebb and flow.

The wild wind joins in this sweet song,
Carrying tales from worlds so strong.
Every wave a chorus, bold and bright,
In twilight's embrace, they take their flight.

Seashells hold whispers of far-off lands,
Stories of mermaids and gentle sands.
In each crest, a promise will arise,
Like the sunrise painting morning skies.

So let us wander, hand in hand,
Along the shore, through golden sand.
Here, beneath the skies so wide,
We'll dance to the ocean's softest tide.

Dances in the Current's Embrace

In the twilight's hush, hearts sway,
Gentle waves sing, night turns to day.
Beneath the moonlight's silver gleam,
Lost in whispers, we drift in a dream.

Flowing like ribbons, the currents call,
A dance of shadows, a spell for all.
With every splash, the sea does spin,
Binding our souls where the light begins.

Nature's pulse, a timeless beat,
Barefoot on shores where land and sea meet.
In the dance of the tide, we find our grace,
Wrapped in the ocean's warm embrace.

Stars above twinkle, secrets share,
As we twirl with the breeze, lost in the air.
We are but wanderers, night's gentle throng,
In the current's rhythm, where we belong.

So let us sway under the starlit sky,
As the waves will carry our dreams up high.
Every heartbeat a promise, a moment's flight,
In the ocean's arms, we find the light.

A Canvas of Stars and Surf

Upon the shore, where dreams ignite,
The ocean shimmers with starlit light.
Waves paint whispers on sandy ground,
In this vast canvas, magic is found.

Each grain of sand holds a tale untold,
Reflections of stories, brave and bold.
The surf's sweet lullaby cradles our fears,
As tides tell legends through laughter and tears.

Stars ignite and spark in the night,
Guiding the lost with their gentle light.
A tapestry woven of dark and bright,
In this cosmic dance, we feel just right.

The salty air drapes the world anew,
As waves embrace all beneath the blue.
With every crest, the universe sings,
And our hearts leap like the wind on its wings.

So let us wander where dreams collide,
With the stars above and the sea as our guide.
For in this moment, vast and free,
We are the artists of our own destiny.

On the Brink of Ocean Dreams

Where the sky touches the deep blue sea,
We stand at the edge, wild and free.
Each wave that crashes, a secret revealed,
An enchanting spell that the ocean had sealed.

Clouds drift lazily, painting the air,
As we gaze upon wonders, beyond compare.
A thrilling breeze whispers tales of old,
In the embrace of the sea, our spirits are bold.

The sun dips low, igniting the tide,
We breathe in the magic, the wildness inside.
Each moment a treasure, each glance a dance,
In the rhythm of waves, the heart finds its chance.

With sandy toes, we forge our path,
The ocean's laughter ignites our wrath.
A canvas of dreams awaits to unfold,
In the silence of night, our souls become gold.

So let us wander where dreams take flight,
On the brink of adventure, in the soft twilight.
With the stars as our witnesses, we dive and soar,
In the ocean of dreams, forever, explore.

Glimmers Through the Sapphire Veil

In depths of azure, where secrets lie,
Glimmers beckon, a soft, sweet sigh.
Through sapphire veils, the whispers swell,
An enchanting beckon, a spell to quell.

The ocean's heart beats a timeless song,
Where currents swirl and tides belong.
Each flicker of light dances in time,
Painting our dreams with rhythm and rhyme.

Underneath the waves, life twinkles bright,
In this underwater realm, pure delight.
With every ripple, old stories rise,
Beneath the surface, hidden empires lie.

Let the gentle tides carry our fears,
As we wade through memories, laughter, and tears.
In these glimmers, our spirits are bound,
By the magic of waves and the beauty they found.

So here we linger in twilight's embrace,
As the ocean unveils its timeless grace.
With hearts intertwined beneath the swell,
In the sapphire veil, we find our spell.

Murmurs of the Tranquil Deep

Beneath the waves, a secret lies,
A gentle hum beneath bright skies.
Silent whispers of the day,
Guide lost sailors on their way.

Corals dance in muted hues,
Tales of old, the ocean's muse.
In this place, the shadows creep,
Where dreams and tides forever sweep.

Starfish lay on silken sand,
A treasure trove at nature's hand.
The bubbles rise, a fleeting thought,
In the depths, such wonders sought.

Moonlight glistens on the crest,
Nature sings, the sea's own jest.
With every swell, a promise dear,
The ocean's heart, forever near.

Lullabies of the Midnight Sea

When twilight wraps the world in veil,
The ocean hums a soothing tale.
Night's soft kiss on waters deep,
Calls forth dreams as sailors sleep.

Starlight weaves through waves so wide,
A silver path, a dreamer's guide.
Crickets chirp a soft refrain,
As echoes of the sea remain.

Each tide brings forth a whispered prayer,
Carried on the salty air.
The sea reflects the moon's embrace,
In every wave, a hidden grace.

Deep beneath, the creatures play,
In shadows where the mermaids sway.
Their laughter mingles with the breeze,
An ageless song among the seas.

Echoes of the Forgotten Waves

In the depths where shadows dwell,
Lies a tale too deep to tell.
Echoes of the past arise,
Beneath the surface, lost in sighs.

Waves that crash with ancient force,
Whispering tales, their timeless source.
A ship once sailed on quivering tides,
Now only where the silence hides.

The sea remembers every fight,
As it swallows both day and night.
In each ripple, history's breath,
A dance of life, or echoes of death.

Glimmers fade in twilight's shade,
Stories of treasures long betrayed.
Yet here amid the ocean's moans,
Lie remnants of forgotten bones.

Woven Dreams on Aquatic Canvas

Upon the tides, a canvas blooms,
Where the sea dictates its tunes.
Brush of waves, with colors bright,
Creating dreams in soft twilight.

Seashells echo in the spray,
While stars above silently sway.
Each ripple forms a tale anew,
Woven dreams, both bold and true.

The currents whisper secrets rare,
In a language beyond compare.
Each brushstroke signifies the grace,
Of the water's endless embrace.

As night descends, the canvas glows,
With soft luminescence that flows.
The ocean's heart, a masterpiece,
Crafted in wonder, never cease.

Shadows Beneath the Moonlit Surface

In the night where whispers dwell,
Shadows dance, a silken spell.
Moonbeams shimmer on the lake,
As secrets stir, the waters wake.

Beneath the surface, dreams take flight,
Glimmers of hope, a haunting light.
Ripples echo tales of yore,
While the world breathes, evermore.

Stars align in a velvet sky,
Unfurling wishes, wafting high.
A symphony of silent sighs,
Beneath the moon, where magic lies.

Echos shimmer, lines intertwine,
Offering truths in a world divine.
The water holds each longing glance,
Ensnared in an ancient trance.

So linger here, O brave, bequeath,
Unlock the dreams that thirst beneath.
For in the night, all is reborn,
In shadows cast, a new morn's sworn.

Ethereal Currents of Enchantment

In the depths where currents weave,
Whispers echo, dreams believe.
Threads of light in twilight's cloak,
Dance like secrets, softly woke.

With every ripple, tales arise,
Of ancient spirits, boundless skies.
They sing of journeys, of lost fate,
And weave their spells to captivate.

A brush of water, cool and clear,
Calls to soul, drawing near.
As moonlit pathways shimmer bright,
Guiding hearts through endless night.

Each glance reflects the stories told,
Of dreams once young that dared be bold.
Through every wave, enchantments flow,
In darkness held, where wonders grow.

The air is thick with whispered charms,
Open arms and beckon calls.
In currents deep, the magic's spun,
As twilight stirs, and day is done.

Beneath the Wavelength of Dreams

At dawn's first blush, where shadows merge,
Wavelengths hum, awaken surge.
A palette bright, of hopes untold,
In the silence, futures unfold.

Beneath the veil of twilight's gleam,
Visions spark like a tender dream.
Footfalls echo on the dew-kissed grass,
Time weaves gently, timeless, alas.

In this space where wishes play,
Hearts entwined, they find their way.
Each sigh, a note in fate's design,
In starlit realms, all souls align.

Undulating echoes of mystic lore,
Entwined in whispers, tales to explore.
Resonating deep in the astral sea,
Where dreams unite, forever free.

So let the waves of possibility swell,
Within this realm, all is well.
A journey begun beneath the twinkle,
Of dreams' embrace, an eternal sprinkle.

The Submerged Symphony of Lost Souls

In the murmur of waves, a symphony sighs,
Lost souls linger beneath the skies.
Each note a whisper, a tale to tell,
Of lives intertwined in the ocean's swell.

Through currents deep and shadows cast,
Fragments of time in the silence amassed.
Echoes of laughter, of joy turned to tears,
Fade into shadows as memory nears.

A haunting melody threads the air,
Binding hearts that once laid bare.
Each ghostly glance, a fleeting chance,
A dance through a dream in a timeless trance.

With every tide, secrets arise,
A chorus of hopes, beneath vast skies.
As the moonlight bathes the world in grace,
Rekindling warmth within each space.

So listen close to the ocean's heart,
Where every note plays a vital part.
In depths where lost souls find their plea,
A symphony echoes, forever free.

Reflections in the Ocean's Mirror

Beneath the waves, the magic sways,
Where silver fish in twilight play.
Stars above, like lanterns glow,
In the ocean's mirror, dreams flow.

Whispers of the deep call forth,
Echoes of sea, a silent mirth.
The tides remind of stories told,
In shimmering currents, treasures bold.

With every pulse, the water sings,
Of mariners, ships, and forgotten things.
Mysteries dance on the ocean's face,
A tapestry woven in time and space.

Glimmers of hope in a darkened sea,
Waves of longing, setting spirits free.
In the twilight, reflections gleam,
The ocean beckons, a tantalizing dream.

And as the sun dips low and sly,
The horizon blushes, the waves sigh.
In this realm where wishes glide,
The ocean's mirror holds worlds inside.

Depths of the Enchanted Abyss

In shadows deep, where wonders dwell,
A realm unfolds, a mystic spell.
Mermaids weave with threads of light,
In the enchanted abyss, dreams take flight.

Coral castles, bathed in hue,
Guard secrets of the ocean blue.
Eerie sounds, like lullabies,
Guide lost souls to where magic lies.

Fathoms dark, a siren's call,
With every wave, the heart enthralls.
Treasured gems in silken sand,
All awaits in this underwater land.

With gentle currents, time stands still,
The ocean's heart, a longing thrill.
Echoing tales of ages past,
Where shadows linger, spells are cast.

In the depths, let your spirit roam,
Find solace in the ocean's home.
For beneath the waves, life's a dance,
In the enchanted abyss, take a chance.

Tides of Forgotten Fantasies

Upon the shore, the memories swell,
Tales whisper low, as waves compel.
Forgotten dreams on the winds do ride,
In the tides, where hopes abide.

Each ebb and flow, a story spins,
Of battles fought, of losses, wins.
The sea remembers, so shall we,
In its embrace, forever free.

Waves like laughter, and sighs like tears,
Echo through the depth of years.
Lost sailors sing to the moon's soft glow,
In forgotten fantasies, we'll learn to flow.

Footprints washed by the tides of time,
Memories linger, like verses in rhyme.
Every splash, a portal to the past,
In this dance, the shadows cast.

So let us wander, hand in hand,
Through the dreams that shape this land.
In the lapping tides, we'll find our way,
To forgotten fantasies where hearts can stay.

The Siren's Lament in Sapphire Tides

In sapphire depths, the siren weeps,
Her haunting song, the ocean keeps.
Melodies of love, loss, and regret,
In the tides, where dreams are set.

Beneath the moon, her voice ascends,
For lonely hearts, her music blends.
With every note, a wish takes flight,
In the twilight glow, hearts ignite.

The ocean whispers her muted cries,
In echoes soft, beneath the skies.
For love once lost in tempest's churn,
A tale of sorrow for which we yearn.

With shimmering scales and tear-streaked cheek,
Her song breathes life to what was bleak.
As waves cascade, her spirit flies,
In the sapphire tides, a world defies.

And when the stars like diamonds shine,
Her lamented tale is forever entwined.
In every ripple, her essence glides,
The siren's heart in sapphire tides.

Ethereal Echoes in Liquid Realms

Beneath the silver sheen of tides,
Mysteries in whispers flow,
As shadows dance where starlight hides,
In depths where moonlit currents glow.

Here, dreams drift softly on the breeze,
Entwined with tales of ancient lore,
Each ripple tells of spirits' pleas,
In realms forever to explore.

A tapestry of light and shade,
Woven where the sea meets sky,
In every pulse, a serenade,
Where phantoms of the deep sigh high.

From echoes bright, the past ignites,
In liquid halls, pure magic breathes,
Where echoes croon of starry nights,
And moonlit paths the ocean weaves.

So listen close, for secrets gleam,
In every wave, a tale takes flight,
A journey spun from thought and dream,
In liquid realms, the world is bright.

Secrets Beneath the Coral Roof

Beneath the vibrant coral reef,
A world awakes in hues so bold,
Where whispers share a gentle grief,
And stories of the deep unfold.

Each crag and crevice holds a key,
To treasures lost in silken waves,
The laughter of the fish runs free,
While shadows guard the ancient graves.

In tangled gardens full of light,
The secrets linger in the throng,
As colors twine and spirits flight,
In harmony, they hum their song.

Anemones sway with graceful ease,
Their tender touch, a lover's peace,
Where time elapses, and hearts release,
The dance of life will never cease.

So dive beneath the coral dome,
Embrace the rhythm of their call,
For in this world, we find a home,
With secrets waiting, one and all.

Shimmers of the Siren's Dream

In twilight's glow, the sirens sing,
With voices sweet as ocean's tide,
They weave enchantments, dreams take wing,
In shimmering depths where shadows hide.

Their laughter sparkles on the foam,
Like diamonds cast on velvet blue,
Each note a promise, far from home,
A lullaby for hearts so true.

The stars above, they gaze and weep,
As moonbeams kiss the tranquil sea,
In dreams, the echoes softly creep,
And every heart yearns to be free.

Through currents swift, their whispers flow,
Enticing sailors with their charm,
Yet hidden dangers lie below,
Where danger waits to sound the alarm.

Yet still they sing, with hope ablaze,
For every heart has tales to weave,
In shimmers bright, we find our ways,
And in their dreams, we dare to believe.

Luminous Waves and Wistful Whispers

In luminous waves that kiss the shore,
The secrets of the ocean rise,
With whispers soft, they long to soar,
And paint the world with vibrant skies.

Each gentle swell, a touch of grace,
Where dreams are born, and wishes flow,
Beneath the stars, a tender trace,
Of longing hearts that drift and go.

In the stillness, tales unfold,
Of sailors brave and lost at sea,
With every wave, a story told,
Of love, of loss, of mystery.

The ebb and flow, a dance divine,
With every tide, a surge of light,
In wistful whispers, hearts entwine,
And shadows bloom in soft moonlight.

So let us gather, hand in hand,
To write our tales in endless rhyme,
In luminous waves, forever stand,
And cherish moments lost in time.

The Dance of Currents and Fates

In twilight's glow, the waters twirl,
Whispers drift like petals' swirl.
The sea's embrace, both soft and bold,
Holds secrets deep, in currents cold.

From depths unknown, a tale unfolds,
Of dreams untold, and hearts of gold.
With every wave, a choice is made,
In moonlit ripples, destinies played.

In shadows cast where shadows roam,
The currents carry tales back home.
A dance of fate upon the foam,
An ocean vast, its wildest poem.

Beneath the crest where starlights gleam,
A shimmering thread ties each dream.
Together they weave in fluid state,
A tapestry rich, the threads of fate.

So in the depths, let your heart sail,
For life, my dear, is but a tale.
The dance of currents, both fierce and light,
Guides us gently into the night.

Tales from the Aqua Labyrinth

In the heart of liquid maze,
Whispers echo, echoes blaze.
Through corridors of azure deep,
Ancient secrets softly creep.

Fish with scales like shards of glass,
Dance beneath where shadows pass.
In every twist, in every bend,
There lurks a story, stark and splendid.

The current flows, a guiding thread,
Carving paths where few have tread.
With every turn, your courage grows,
As magic in the water flows.

The labyrinth hums a lullaby,
To dreams that drift and memories fly.
In stillness deep, in currents wide,
The tales await, with arms spread wide.

From the depths, with hidden glee,
The aqua maze calls out to thee.
A quest for truth, a journey's song,
In woven waters, where you belong.

Beneath the Surface: Dreamscapes of the Sea

Beneath the waves, a world awakes,
In shimmering hues, the silence breaks.
Dreamscapes linger where shadows play,
In depths where sunlight fades away.

Coral castles rise and fall,
In gentle sway, they heed the call.
A ballet of creatures, lost in trance,
Each flick of fin, a fleeting dance.

Entities of the ocean's lore,
Whisper secrets, forevermore.
In dreamlike states, we drift and glide,
With tender waves that beckon wide.

The surface glistens, hides the deep,
Where ancient stories yearn to sleep.
In every bubble, in every sigh,
A memory whispers, a silent cry.

So close your eyes and feel the flow,
Dive deeper still, let the currents show.
In this vast sea, your heart will roam,
Beneath the surface, find your home.

Siren's Call Amidst the Tidal Flow

In twilight's hush, a song resounds,
A siren's call through ocean bounds.
With haunting notes that weave and wind,
A melody, both sweet and blind.

The tides respond, in rhythmic sway,
Enticing souls to drift away.
With fleeting whispers of the sea,
Come dance with shadows, fleetingly.

The moonlight bathes the restless tide,
A dreamy veil, where secrets hide.
Each pulse of water, a siren's breath,
Lures the weary, flirts with death.

Yet listen closely, heed the sound,
For in the depths, your fate is found.
The call of waves, both true and false,
Can lead to joy or lead to loss.

So linger not on gentle shores,
The siren's song forever soars.
Embrace the current, brave the flow,
In tidal dances, let dreams grow.

Shimmering Pathways of the Deep

Beneath the waves, a dance begins,
Where light and water entwine their sins,
Each ripple whispers ancient tales,
Of sunken dreams and ghostly sails.

The coral blooms in vibrant hues,
A symphony of life imbues,
In every crevice, secrets lie,
Beneath the vast and endless sky.

The fish dart by in playful chase,
In this enchanted, silent place,
With every heartbeat of the sea,
A rhythm that sets spirits free.

Yet shadows loom, and thoughts may drift,
Through currents deep, the tides may shift,
What wonders dwell where few may roam,
In underwater realms, our home.

So let us dive into the blue,
Explore the depths, both old and new,
For in the depths, our hearts will see,
The magic lives in you and me.

The Call of Distant Shores

Across the waves, a whisper calls,
From far-off lands where adventure sprawls,
The scent of salt, the taste of dreams,
In every echo, hope redeems.

The sails unfurl beneath the sun,
Each journey taken, a story spun,
As gulls take wing, the heart takes flight,
Guided by stars in the velvet night.

Among the seas, a treasure waits,
In mirrored depths and hidden gates,
With every stroke, the past unfolds,
In tapestry of tales retold.

Yet storms may rise and skies may grey,
The call remains to seize the day,
For in the tempest's wild embrace,
Lies strength and courage we must face.

So let us journey, hand in hand,
To distant shores, a magic land,
And with each wave, our spirits soar,
Forever drawn to oceans' roar.

Soliloquy of the Shy Tide

The tide ebbs gently, shy and slow,
Whispering secrets only it knows,
As soft sand cradles the fleeting kiss,
Of moments lost in ocean's bliss.

Each wave's retreat, a longing sigh,
A tale of love that dares not lie,
In rhythms sweet, the heart will dare,
To dream of kisses lost in air.

The moonbeams dance on waters wide,
In twilight's glow, the night will bide,
And in the hush of silver light,
A serenade takes flight in night.

So let the tides sing soft and low,
The song of life, the ebb and flow,
For in this dance, we find our way,
To hope anew with each new day.

Thus in the silence, heartbeats find,
Connection deep, a love entwined,
And as the shy tide draws away,
New wonders wait with break of day.

The Melancholy of Swells and Shadows

When ocean swells in twilight's haze,
A tale of sorrow, a wistful gaze,
The shadows stretch upon the foam,
In depths unknown, we seek a home.

Each wave that crashes speaks of loss,
The weight of dreams, the silent cross,
Yet in the breaking, hope does rise,
To kiss the shores with gentle sighs.

The gulls cry out in lonely flight,
As darkened clouds obscure the light,
But still the sea, with endless grace,
Embraces all in warm embrace.

And when the night enfolds the shore,
The heart will ache, but yearn for more,
For in the shadows, truths revealed,
A deeper bond that must be healed.

So let the swells and shadows blend,
In harmony where dreams transcend,
For every heart must learn to brave,
The storms of life, the love we crave.

Whispers of the Siren's Echo

In twilight's hush, soft echoes sing,
Where shadows weave and dim lights cling,
A haunting call floats on the breeze,
Enticing hearts like gentle seas.

Beneath the moon, the waters gleam,
With silver threads that weave a dream,
Each note a lure, a sweet embrace,
To guide the lost in darkened space.

Yet heed the warning in the song,
For beauty hides where sirens throng,
With every glance to deepened blue,
A peril waits for hearts anew.

They dance on waves, a mystic view,
Unraveling paths few ever knew,
In tangled foam, their secrets sleep,
Where promises are buried deep.

So tread with care, oh curious soul,
For every heart might pay the toll,
In whispers soft, their truths entwine
The siren's song, forever blind

Reflections on the Shimmering Tide

The tide rolls in, a mirror bright,
Glistening hues of day and night,
With secrets spun in swirling lines,
Where every crest, a tale confides.

Upon the shore, dreams drift like sand,
In fleeting moments, all unplanned,
Reflections dance, a fleeting sight,
Timeless wishes caught in light.

Each wave that crashes, soft and sweet,
Whispers of journeys, bittersweet,
The ebb and flow, a gentle guide,
Reminds us of the paths we ride.

Beneath the stars, beneath the glow,
The shimmering tide begins to flow,
It carries hopes to distant lands,
And cradles dreams in its soft hands.

So cast your gaze on waters wide,
And listen close to the ocean's tide,
For every crest holds stories grand,
Reflections not in grains of sand.

Luminous Currents of Forgotten Dreams

Beneath the surface, shadows play,
In currents where the lost dreams sway,
With glimmers faint, they drift and glide,
In whispered hopes, they softly bide.

Once vibrant thoughts that shone so bright,
Now dance in darkness, void of light,
Yet still they pulse in depths unknown,
In every wave, their seeds are sown.

The essence of what could have been,
Keeps echoing in waters keen,
For every heart that dared to wish,
Lingers somewhere in the abyss.

With tides that pull and tides that break,
Lost dreams awaken from their ache,
To shimmer softly on the face,
Of waters deep, a sacred space.

So dive down deep where silence reigns,
And find the joy amidst the pains,
For in those currents, brightly gleams,
The luminous light of faded dreams.

Secrets Beneath the Celestial Waves

Underneath the velvet sky,
Where starlit dreams and whispers lie,
The ocean holds in its embrace,
A tapestry of time and space.

Each wave a story, ancient, wise,
In depths unseen, where silence sighs,
The secrets woven, thread by thread,
Are whispered softly, long since said.

With every moonrise, tales unfold,
Of treasures lost and wanderers bold,
In watery graves, their myths remain,
In ceaseless cycles of joy and pain.

So let the tide wash over fears,
Embrace the magic held for years,
For in the depths, the past will weave,
A fabric rich, one must believe.

So sail through starlit oceans wide,
Where mysteries and beauty tide,
For every wave sings, every crest,
Beneath celestial waves, we rest.

The Mermaid's Glistening Haunt

In caverns deep, where shadows play,
The mermaids weave their songs each day.
With scales that shimmer, bright like stars,
They beckon sailors from afar.

The waves caress the jagged rocks,
As whispers drift, like ticking clocks.
A dance of light, so soft and rare,
In water's grasp, they spin through air.

With hair like silk and laughter sweet,
They draw you in, a siren's feat.
In dreams, you find their glistening hall,
Where every secret waits to call.

Yet heed the tales of olden lore,
For love with them may mean much more.
A heart entwined in ocean's throne,
Shall find its echo, forever known.

So ponder well, brave souls at sea,
For enchantments hold both trap and glee.
The mermaid's haunt, a haunting song,
Will lead you where the lost belong.

Lullabies of the Sunken Moon

Beneath the tides, a lullaby,
The moonlit whispers stir and sigh.
In watery realms where shadows hide,
The echoes of the night collide.

With silver trails, the fish dart swift,
In liquid dreams, the currents shift.
They waltz beneath the starlit sheen,
In haunting beauty, soft and serene.

The sunken treasures of olden days,
Glisten softly in lunar rays.
Each heartbeat thrums with ancient tales,
Of ships long lost, of haunted sails.

A serenade from depths below,
Where sailors once did bravely row.
In evening's grasp, the waves now croon,
Sweet lullabies of the sunken moon.

So find your peace in twilight's grasp,
And let the ocean's lullabies clasp.
For in their arms, all fears dissolve,
And restless hearts shall find resolve.

Ethereal Glimmers in the Deep Blue

In twilight's glow, the waters gleam,
With ethereal glimmers, a wisp of dream.
Beneath the surface, secrets dwell,
In silken whispers, their stories swell.

Fish painted bright, a dance of hues,
Through tangled forests in gentle muse.
Their laughter twinkles, a playful spark,
In labyrinths lost, where shadows dark.

Anemones sway, with grace and flair,
In colors bold, they pirouette rare.
From coral castles, a kingdom shy,
Drawn forever to the ocean's sigh.

Each ripple sings of things unseen,
A magic thrums in cerulean green.
The depths unveil their mystic art,
A symphony that stirs the heart.

So wander forth where waters churn,
Let the call of the deep make you yearn.
For in those glimmers lies a key,
To worlds where dreams and waters free.

Chasing Shadows of Aquatic Reveries

Through twilight hues where shadows play,
The dreams of water drift away.
In currents strong, they slip and swirl,
As echoes weave, and memories twirl.

Upon the waves, a silhouette,
A dance of hope, a sweet duet.
With every splash, a tale retold,
Of sunlit days and spirits bold.

The gurgling laugh of bubbling streams,
Holds all the promise of secret dreams.
With fins like silver, they glide and dart,
Breaking the surface, a work of art.

Yet delve into the deeper blue,
Where shadows whisper, secrets true.
Where phantoms of the deep reside,
And currents shift, like time's divide.

Chase those shadows, oh longing soul,
In watery realms, find the whole.
For every ripple, every sigh,
Holds the essence of the sky.

The Ocean's Heartbeat in Solitude

In the still of night, waves sigh,
Whispers of dreams, beneath the sky.
Moonlit paths on frothy crests,
The ocean's heart, it quietly rests.

Shells scattered like memories lost,
Each grain of sand, a tale embossed.
The tide pulls back, a lover's retreat,
In solitude, the sea's heartbeat.

Stars twinkle soft, a silent choir,
Kindling the waves, a gentle fire.
Breath of the deep, a lullaby sweet,
Cradled in darkness, time feels complete.

No land in sight, just endless blue,
A world apart, known by few.
In solitude's grasp, the ocean sways,
Eternity danced in foamy bays.

Each ripple a story, each wave its part,
The ocean's pulse, a tender heart.
In the vast expanse, I find my way,
To listen close to the waves' ballet.

Tides of Time and Forgotten Sailors

Waves whisper softly of tales untold,
Of sailors brave and hearts of gold.
Crafted from dreams, they sailed afar,
Chasing the wind and the evening star.

Time's gentle hand tugs at the shore,
With each passing tide, we remember more.
Ghosts of the past in the sea breeze glide,
Echoes of laughter where secrets hide.

Salt-kissed memories, they rise and fall,
Voices of sailors, a haunting call.
With every ripple, their spirits roam,
Bound to the ocean, forever home.

Beneath the waves, forgotten dreams,
Sip from the ocean's endless streams.
Ink of the sea, the shanties weave,
Stories of sailors who dared to believe.

In twilight's glow, their legends ignite,
With every tide, they take flight.
The moon watches over, serene and bright,
Guiding the souls to a harbor of light.

Beneath the Velvet Sea

Beneath the velvet, the sea lies still,
A cradle of dreams and twilight thrill.
Fish dart like shadows, weaving grace,
In the depths where time leaves no trace.

Coral gardens, vibrant and rare,
Whispers of life in the salty air.
Songs of the ocean, ancient and deep,
Secrets are held in its tranquil sweep.

The sway of the tide, a gentle dance,
Entwined with shadows in a timeless trance.
From the surface shimmering in light,
To whispering depths that call in the night.

In silence, the currents embrace the past,
Where echoes of voices forever last.
Beneath the velvet, the stories flow,
A realm of wonder, where dreams can grow.

As day meets the dusk, a canvas unfurls,
With shades of mystery, the ocean twirls.
Beneath its surface, where magic lies,
The velvet sea breathes, beneath stormy skies.

Currents of Celestial Echoes

In the cradle of night, the sea calls forth,
Currents of whispers, from south to north.
Stars shimmer softly on water's face,
Mirroring dreams in a cosmic embrace.

Tales of the ancients ride on the breeze,
Tides of forgotten, flow with such ease.
Every splash holds a celestial truth,
A journey of wisdom, the fountain of youth.

In liquid horizons, the cosmos unfolds,
With secrets of ages, both new and old.
The moon's silver glow, a guiding light,
Beckoning all towards the infinite night.

Beneath the surface, the world holds sway,
Echoes of starlight, a shimmering ray.
Currents of stories that weave in the dark,
Charting the heavens, igniting a spark.

With tides of emotion, the ocean breathes,
Embracing the night as it gently weaves.
Currents of echoes, celestial streams,
Cradle the heart in the realm of dreams.

The Mystery of the Aquatic Dreamscape

Beneath the waves where secrets swirl,
A world unfolds, a mystic whirl.
In currents deep, the shadows play,
Whispers of dreams that drift away.

Mysterious lights in dark embrace,
Call forth the heart to join the chase.
Echoes of laughter ride the foam,
In the aquatic dreamscape, we roam.

Each petal of seaweed tells a tale,
Of ancient ships and a ghostly wail.
The sirens hum, a soft lament,
In waters where the time is bent.

With every rise and every fall,
The ocean breathes, it heeds the call.
To wander here is to understand,
The dreamscape's lure, a mystic land.

So hold your breath and dive beneath,
For in the depths, you'll find belief.
In shimmering pools of cerulean hue,
The aquatic dreamscape waits for you.

Chasing Reflections in Tidal Waters

When the sun sets low and shadows bloom,
The tide reveals its mirrored gloom.
Reflections dance upon the shore,
A fleeting glimpse, forevermore.

Each wave that crashes sings a song,
Of fleeting moments woven strong.
Chasing reflections, we find our place,
In the tidal waters' soft embrace.

Among the shells and shimmering grains,
Echoes of laughter still remain.
Ghosts of the past in each ripple's play,
Guide us gently on our way.

As night descends with stars afire,
The ocean whispers, stokes desire.
To chase reflections, we lose our fears,
In tidal waters, we drown our tears.

So let the moonlight lead us near,
To where the heart knows no more fear.
In chasing dreams that surf the tide,
We find the places where hopes abide.

The Haunting Melody of Ocean Abandon

Lonely waves crash on barren shores,
Where the ocean's heart silently pours.
In the wind's wail, a haunting tune,
Echoes beneath the ghostly moon.

Wreckage tells of journeys lost,
Each splintered mast, a bitter cost.
The melody drifts on salted air,
Whispers of shipmates, lost in despair.

Tales of mariners who braved the storm,
Now lie beneath, in dreams reborn.
Their voices rise like the tides that swell,
In tunes of sorrow, they weave their spell.

The ocean's embrace, both fierce and wide,
Holds memories where dreams abide.
Through echoing songs, their spirits soar,
In the haunting melody, forevermore.

A symphony played by the sea so grand,
Reminds us of journeys, both planned and unplanned.
So listen closely, and you may hear,
The melody of love, loss, and fear.

Beneath the Glistening Tide

In twilight's glow, the waters gleam,
A hidden world where visions teem.
Beneath the glistening tide, we dive,
Into the magic that's alive.

Coral castles touch the sky,
As fish like jewels flit swiftly by.
In secret grottos, secrets lie,
Beneath the waves, where dreams won't die.

The whispers of the ocean breeze,
Urge us softly, bring us to our knees.
With every ripple, every sway,
The glistening tide calls us to play.

Anemones bloom, stars in the night,
Guiding the lost with their soft light.
In waters where the heart takes flight,
Beneath the glistening tide, all feels right.

So venture forth, let spirits glide,
Into the depths where dreams reside.
For in the ocean's tender arms,
We find our peace, our hidden charms.

Celestial Fables of Ocean's Grace

Beneath the stars where dolphins play,
A silver moon whispers songs of sway,
Waves weave tales from days gone by,
Carried forth on a seabird's cry.

The lighthouse beams, a guiding light,
Casting shadows on the endless night,
Mermaids dance in the foamy spray,
Their laughter echoes, fading away.

Secrets sleep in the deep blue sea,
Nurtured by the dreams of what could be,
Tides swirl gently, a rhythmic hymn,
Embracing echoes of times grown dim.

Upon the shore where soft winds sigh,
The ocean tells its vast goodbye,
With every curl and every crest,
It holds the fables of the blessed.

In twilight's glow, the waters gleam,
Reflecting whispers of a distant dream,
For in these depths, the world unfurls,
A tapestry of pearls and swirls.

The Enchanted Tides of Lost Lore

At dawn's first light, the ocean wakes,
With hidden truths and ancient stakes,
Mirrors of time, a tale to weave,
In every wave, the past believes.

Seashells whisper to those who dare,
Of battles fought and love laid bare,
Coral castles, grand and old,
Guard stories waiting to be told.

The wind, a bard with a sailor's grin,
Carries legends of the deep within,
Alluring sirens sing their plight,
Fates entwined in moonlit night.

Upon the sands, the footprints fade,
Each step a memory, each choice made,
Oceans embrace, both fierce and kind,
While time weaves silence, intertwined.

Roads of currents twist and turn,
Through hidden paths, the ancients yearn,
For in the ebb and flow of sea,
The lighthouse stands as history.

Crystal Whirlpools and Phantom Ships

Beneath the surface, shadows play,
Phantom ships in a watery ballet,
Whirlpools swirl with stories spun,
Of sailors lost 'neath the setting sun.

Emerging soft from the ocean's grasp,
Dreams of adventure in a fleeting clasp,
Eerie lights through the depths they gleam,
Guiding souls toward an unseen dream.

In treacherous tides, the waters churn,
As mysteries entwine and secrets burn,
Each ripple sings of that fateful night,
When stars above lost their guiding light.

With hopes aflame, the journeys call,
Yet fear holds fast, a silent wall,
As crystal whirlpools spin the fate,
Of those who wander the haunted slate.

Under the waves where legends dwell,
The secrets of the ocean swell,
In silence deep, the past remains,
A symphony of joyful pains.

Beneath the Surface of Siren's Call

When night descends and shadows creep,
The siren's song disrupts the deep,
Enchanting hearts, a spell so rare,
Leading many into despair.

From rocky shores, the sailors plead,
Against the pull of a darkened need,
For in the depths where echoes play,
Lies a fate none can dismay.

With every note, a promise made,
Of love and loss in ocean's shade,
A haunting beauty, vast and cold,
Wrapped in legends yet untold.

Beneath the waves lies a hidden door,
To worlds unknown on a distant shore,
Where dreams entwine in a tempest's churn,
And the weary hearts forever yearn.

So heed the call of the ocean's sway,
And tread with care on the foamy spray,
For in the depths, the stories shine,
A siren's song, alluring, divine.

Enchanted Waters: Myths of the Abyss

In depths where shadows creep and dwell,
The whispers of lost tales they tell.
Creatures dark, in the inky void,
Guard secrets long, forever cloyed.

The silvery fish that dance through gloom,
Hold stories deep in the ocean's womb.
Fables spun from the ocean's haze,
Enchanted waters, a mystic maze.

Along the shore, soft waves do sigh,
Casting echoes of a long-lost cry.
Mermaids combing their locks of gold,
With secrets of the abyss retold.

In twilight's glow, the sea sparkles bright,
A cloak of stars in the velvet night.
The tides carry dreams, both lost and found,
In enchanted waters, magic is bound.

So heed the tales the currents weave,
In each splash, a memory we leave.
For in the depths, where the shadows lie,
Myths of the abyss will never die.

Beyond the Tides: Horizons of Wonder

Beyond the tides, a world unfold,
With waves of silver and sands of gold.
Each cresting swell holds secrets untold,
Of treasures hidden, and adventures bold.

The horizon beckons with calls of delight,
Whispers of magic in the moonlight bright.
Where sailors venture, their hearts set free,
To explore the realms of the deep, blue sea.

In playful currents, the dolphins glide,
Their joy and laughter, an endless tide.
In whirlpools vast, and calm bays wide,
Horizons of wonder forever abide.

Beneath the waves, a kingdom thrives,
In coral gardens, the ocean jives.
With colors bright, like dreams unfurled,
Beyond the tides, a magical world.

From shipwrecks old to island shores,
Each journey unfolds, as adventure pours.
In the hearts of dreamers, hopes still soar,
Beyond the tides, forevermore.

Reflections of Time in Aquatic Dreams

In tranquil depths, where silence reigns,
Reflections dance, shedding old chains.
The water's mirror holds stories dear,
Of ages past, where dreams draw near.

Aquatic dreams in a liquid trance,
Entwine like phantoms in a mystical dance.
Echoes of laughter, of love and woe,
Flow through the currents, whispering low.

Time flows gently, like a river's song,
A tapestry woven, where we all belong.
In each ripple lies an ember's glow,
Reflections of life in the ebb and flow.

The shadows play games beneath the tide,
With memories flickering, like stars that bide.
In depths of silence, secrets will weave,
Reflections of time, we dare to believe.

So close your eyes and surrender your fears,
Let the waves cradle you, dry your tears.
For in aquatic dreams, we will find,
The depths of our hearts, forever entwined.

Caresses of the Selkie's Touch

Beneath the moon, where the waters gleam,
A tale of enchantment flows like a dream.
Selkies emerging from foam and spray,
With whispers of night that beckon to play.

Their voices linger, a haunting call,
With echoes that dance in the ocean's thrall.
In their embrace, the world melts away,
Caresses of magic, where mortals sway.

Glimmers of skin, as soft as the night,
Transform the shore with ethereal light.
Draped in the mist, they glisten and glide,
Caresses of the selkie, where hearts collide.

From distant shores, they whisper and tease,
Enchanting the waves with rhythmic ease.
In twilight's grace, they spin and twirl,
Caresses of wonder in ocean's whirl.

With every ripple, a soul is adrift,
In selkie's gaze, one finds a gift.
So dance on the shore, let the night unfold,
In caresses of the selkie, stories retold.

Embrace the magic, don't fear the unknown,
For in the depths, true love is sown.
Caresses of the selkie, a heart's longing touch,
In the arms of the ocean, we find so much.

www.ingramcontent.com/pod-product-compliance
Ingram Content Group UK Ltd.
Pitfield, Milton Keynes, MK11 3LW, UK
UKHW021522280125
4335UKWH00036B/963